100 SOLO
CLARINET

Order No. AM 33689
International Standard Book Number: 0.8256.1097.4

Exclusive Distributors:
Music Sales Corporation
257 Park Avenue South, New York, NY 10010 USA
Music Sales Limited
8/9 Frith Street, London W1V 5TZ England
Music Sales Pty. Limited
120 Rothschild Street, Rosebery, Sydney, NSW 2018, Australia

Printed in the United States of America by
Vicks Lithograph and Printing Corporation

100 SOLOS
CLARINET

&

Amsco Publications
London/New York/Sydney

EDELWEISS (FROM "THE SOUND OF MUSIC").

Words by Oscar Hammerstein II. Music by Richard Rodgers.

PICK A POCKET OR TWO (FROM THE COLUMBIA PICTURES-ROMULUS FILM "OLIVER!").

Words and Music by Lionel Bart

SAILING.
Words and Music by Gavin Sutherland.

Slow Beat

MORNING HAS BROKEN.

Words by Eleanor Farleon Music (adaption) by Cat Stevens.

AMAZING GRACE.

Traditional.

Slowly

REVIEWING THE SITUATION (FROM THE COLUMBIA PICTURES-ROMULUS FILM "OLIVER!").

Words and Music by Lionel Bart.

SMILE.

Words by John Turner and Geoffrey Parsons. Music by Charles Chaplin.

Andante

GREENSLEEVES.

Traditional.

Moderato

Da Capo al Fine

DAYS OF WINE AND ROSES.

Words by Johnny Mercer. Music by Henry Mancini.

NEVER SMILE AT A CROCODILE.

Words by Jack Lawrence. Music by Frank Churchill.

Moderately slow and liltingly

PAPER ROSES.
Words and Music by F. Spielman and J. Torre.

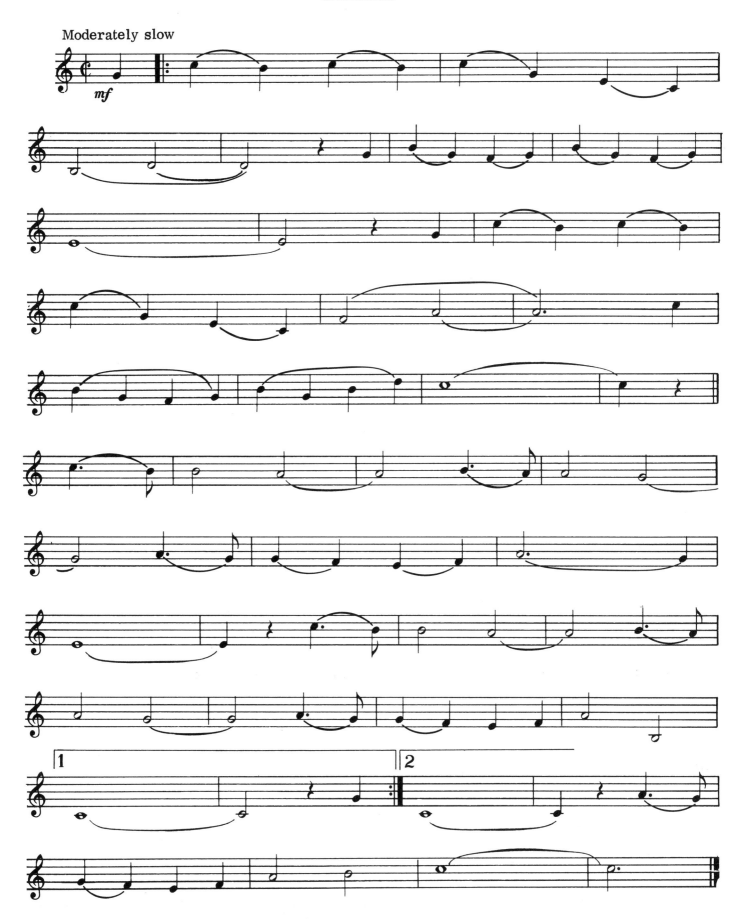

THE DRUNKEN SAILOR.

Traditional.

SHALL WE DANCE (FROM "THE KING AND I").

Words by Oscar Hammerstein. Music by Richard Rodgers.

THEME FROM A SUMMER PLACE.

Words by Mack Discant. Music by Max Steiner.

SHE'S LEAVING HOME.

Words and Music by John Lennon and Paul McCartney.

STREETS OF LONDON.
Words and Music by Ralph McTell.

Moderately fast

WHEN THE SAINTS GO MARCHING IN.

Traditional

Quick march tempo

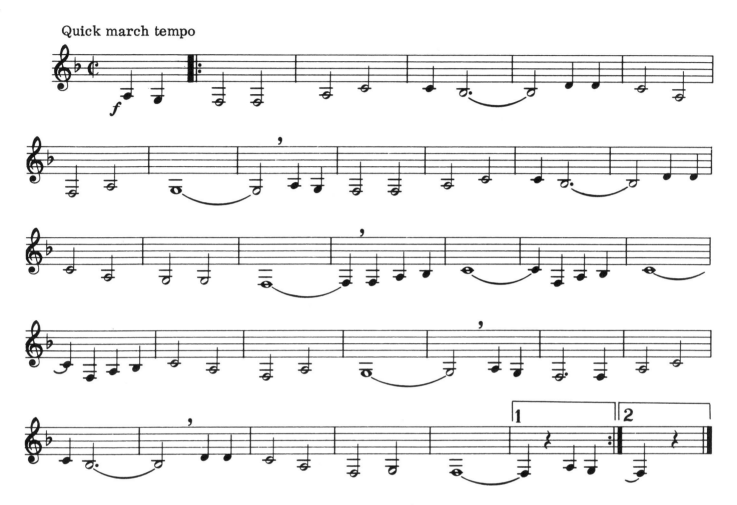

SHENANDOAH.

Traditional.

Flowingly

STRAWBERRY FIELDS FOREVER.

Words and Music by John Lennon and Paul McCartney.

BE BACK SOON (FROM THE COLUMBIA PICTURES-ROMULUS FILM "OLIVER!").

Words and Music by Lionel Bart.

SUPERCALIFRAGILISTICEXPIALIDOCIOUS.
Words and Music by Richard M. Sherman and Robert B. Sherman.

WHO DO YOU THINK YOU'RE KIDDING, MR.HITLER?

Words by Jimmy Perry. Music by Jimmy Perry and Derek Taverner.

CONSIDER YOURSELF (FROM THE COLUMBIA PICTURES-ROMULUS FILM "OLIVER!").

Words and Music by Lionel Bart.

BALI HA'I (FROM "SOUTH PACIFIC").
Words by Oscar Hammerstein II. Music by Richard Rodgers.

LITTLE BROWN JUG.

Traditional.

WHATEVER WILL BE WILL BE (QUE SERA, SERA).

Words and Music by Jay Livingston and Ray Evans.

Moderate waltz

OOM-PAH-PAH (FROM THE COLUMBIA PICTURES-ROMULUS FILM "OLIVER!").

Words and Music by Lionel Bart.

DO-RE-MI.

Words by Oscar Hammerstein II. Music by Richard Rodgers.

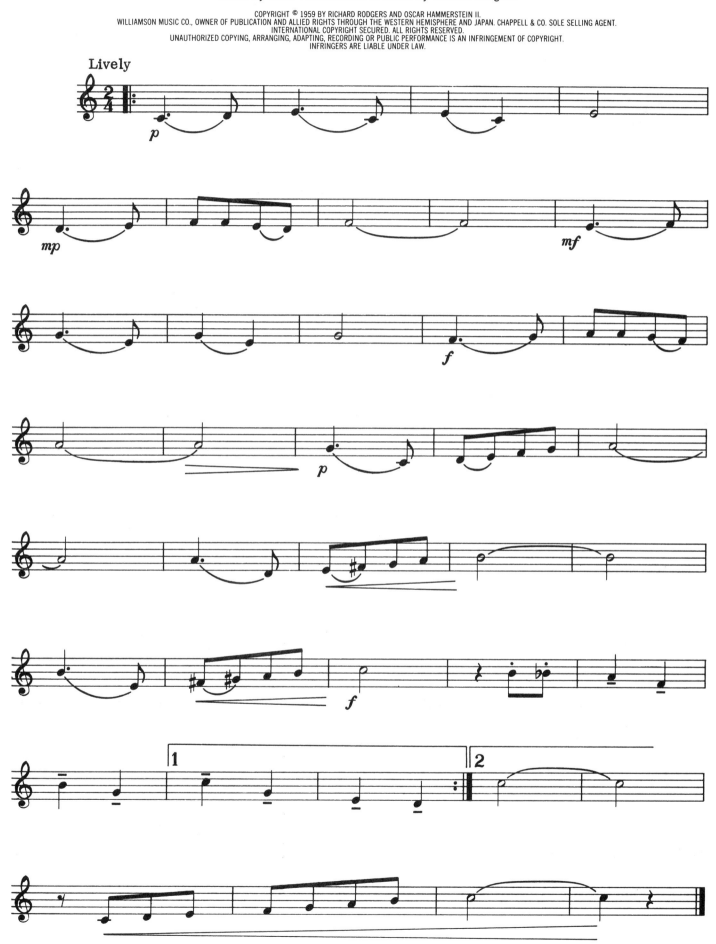

OH, WHAT A BEAUTIFUL MORNING.

Words by Oscar Hammerstein II. Music by Richard Rodgers.

WHERE IS LOVE (FROM THE COLUMBIA PICTURES-ROMULUS FILM "OLIVER").

Words and Music by Lionel Bart.

THE SOUND OF MUSIC.

Words by Oscar Hammerstein II. Music by Richard Rodgers.

JUST FOR YOU.

Words and Music by Alan Price.

SEA OF HEARTBREAK.

Words and Music by Hal David and Paul Hampton.

Moderately bright

OKLAHOMA.

Words by Oscar Hammerstein. Music by Richard Rodgers.

SHE LOVES YOU.

Words and Music by John Lennon & Paul McCartney.

Moderato

I ENJOY BEING A GIRL.

Words by Oscar Hammerstein II. Music by Richard Rodgers.

AS LONG AS HE NEEDS ME (FROM THE COLUMBIA PICTURES-ROMULUS FILM "OLIVER!")

Words and Music by Lionel Bart.

Moderato

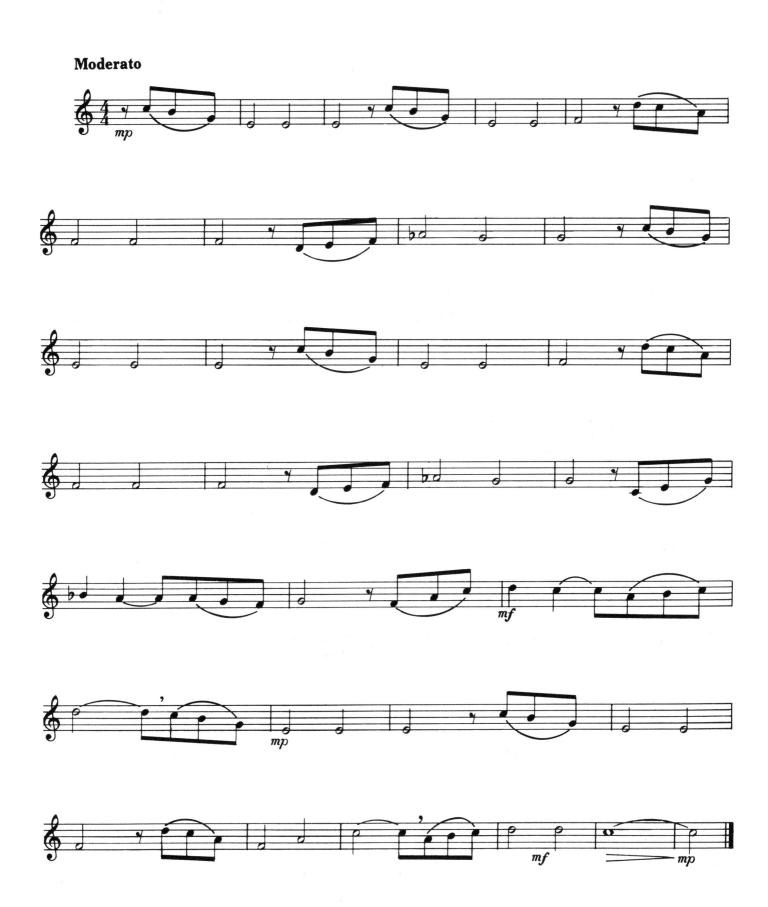

I'D LIKE TO TEACH THE WORLD TO SING.

Words and Music by Roger Cook, Roger Greenaway, Billy Backer and Billy Davis.

Moderato

MICHELLE.
Words and Music by John Lennon and Paul McCartney.

WHEN I'M SIXTY FOUR.

Words and Music by John Lennon and Paul McCartney.

STEPTOE AND SON.

Music by Ron Grainer.

I DON'T KNOW HOW TO LOVE HIM.

Words by Tim Rice. Music by Andrew Lloyd Webber.

KISS ME HONEY-HONEY (KISS ME).

Words and Music by Al Timothy & Michael Julien.

THE RAKES OF MALLOW.

Traditional.

ENGLISH COUNTRY GARDEN.

Traditional.

THE HAWAIIAN WEDDING SONG.

English Words by Al Hoffman and Dick Manning. Hawaiian Words and Music by Charles E. King.

BYE BYE BABY.

Words and Music by Leo Robin and Jule Styne.

NORWEGIAN WOOD.
Words and Music by John Lennon and Paul McCartney.

ALL MY LOVING.
Words and Music by John Lennon and Paul McCartney.

IF I WERE A RICH MAN.

Words by Sheldon Harnick. Music by Jerry Bock.

Moderate lilt

HAPPY TALK (FROM "SOUTH PACIFIC").

Words by Oscar Hammerstein II. Music by Richardd Rodgers.

THERE IS NOTHING LIKE A DAME (FROM "SOUTH PACIFIC").

Words by Oscar Hammerstein II. Music by Richard Rodgers.

DON'T CRY FOR ME ARGENTINA.

Lyrics by Tim Rice. Music by Andrew Lloyd Webber.

PEOPLE WILL SAY WE'RE IN LOVE.

Words by Oscar Hammerstein. Music by Richard Rodgers.

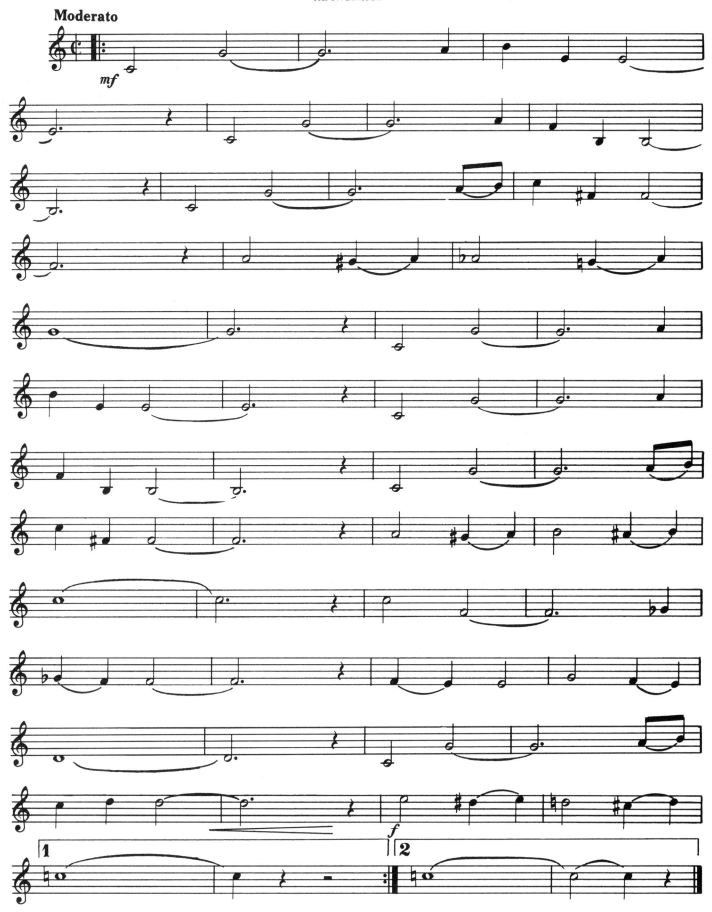

CLIMB EVERY MOUNTAIN.
Words by Oscar Hammerstein II. Music by Richard Rodgers.

FOOD GLORIOUS FOOD (FROM THE COLUMBIA PICTURES-ROMULUS FILM "OLIVER!").

Words and Music by Lionel Bart.

THIS OLE HOUSE.
Words and Music by Stuart Hamblen.

WHO WILL BUY? (FROM THE COLUMBIA PICTURES-ROMULUS FILM "OLIVER!").

Words and Music by Lionel Bart.

IT'S NOT UNUSUAL.

Words and Music by Gordon Mills & Les Reed.

Moderately, with a beat

HOW INSENSITIVE.

Music by Antonio Carlos Jobim. Original lyrics by Vinicius De Moraes. English lyrics by Norman Gimbel.

Moderately slow

DOWNTOWN.
Words and Music by Tony Hatch.

THE DEADWOOD STAGE (WHIP-CRACK-AWAY).

Music by Sammy Fain. Lyric by Paul Francis Webster.

WITH A LITTLE HELP FROM MY FRIENDS.

Words and Music by John Lennon & Paul McCartney.

MONEY MONEY MONEY.

Words and Music by Benny Andersson and Bjorn Ulvaeus.

Moderato

WATERLOO.

Words and Music by Benny Andersson, Stig Anderson and Bjorn Ulvaeus.

THE ENTERTAINER.

Scott Joplin.

DANCING QUEEN.

Words and Music by Benny Andersson, Stig Anderson and Bjorn Ulvaeus.

BLUESETTE.

Words by Norman Gimbel. Music by John Thielemans.

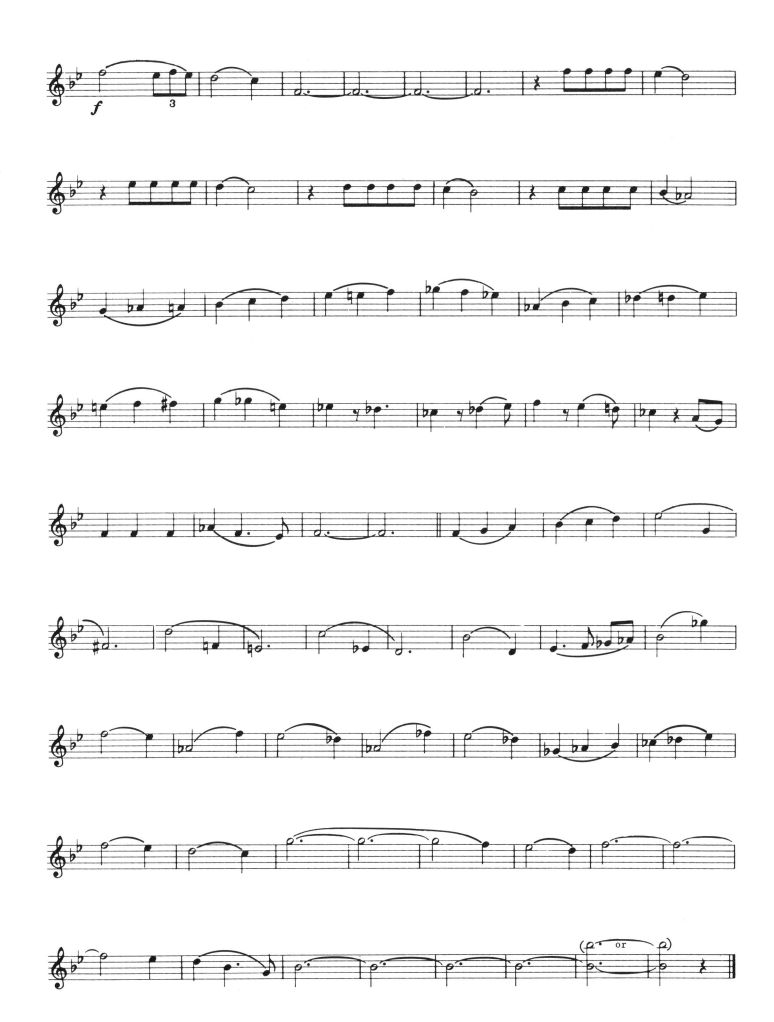

THE GIRL FROM IPANEMA.

Music by Antonio Carlos Jobim. English Words by Norman Gimbel. Original Words by Vinicius De Moraez.

Moderately slow

TUXEDO JUNCTION.

Words and Music by J. Dash, E. Hawkins, W. Johnson, B. Feyne.

NOLA.
Traditional.

Schottische tempo

AH, SO PURE (MARTHA).

von Flotow.

ANDANTE FROM FIFTH SYMPHONY.

Peter Tchaikovsky.

BOURRÉE.

Johann Krieger.

LA CI DAREM LA MANO.

W.A. Mozart.

BARCAROLLE.

Offenbach.

GAVOTTE.

Gossec.

FINALE FROM SYMPHONY NO. 1

Johannes Brahms.

LAMENT.

Bela Bartok.

MINUET IN G.

Beethoven.

MUSETTE.

Johann Sebastian Bach.

Andante pastorale

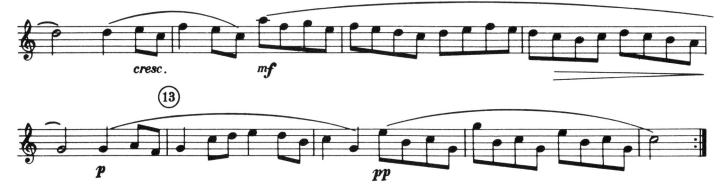

NOCTURNE.

Frederic Chopin.

Andante

IRISH WASHERWOMAN.

Traditional.

ARKANSAS TRAVELLER.

Traditional.

POP GOES THE WEASEL.

Traditional.

BLOW THE MAN DOWN.

Traditional.

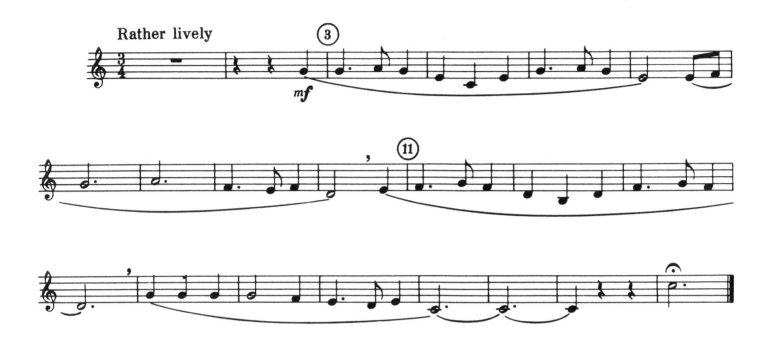

RED RIVER VALLEY.

Cowboy Song.

RONDINO.

W.A. Mozart.

KERRY DANCE.
Traditional.

SAILOR'S HORNPIPE.
Traditional.

FISHER'S HORNPIPE.
Traditional.

BLACK IS THE COLOR (OF MY TRUE LOVE'S HAIR).

Traditional.

Slowly

SARABANDE.

Arcangelo Carelli.

Lento espressivo

SCARBOROUGH FAIR.

Traditional.

TAMBOURIN.

Jean-Phillippe Rameau.

GERMAN DANCE.

Beethoven.

THE TROUT.

Franz Schubert.

MELODY IN F.

Rubinstein.

NONE BUT THE LONELY HEART.

Tchaikovsky.

BEAUTIFUL DREAMER.

Stephen Foster.